The Curious Sexual
Adventure
of the Reverend
John Prince

For the Worthies
of Devon

The Curious Sexual Adventure *of the* Reverend John Prince

As observed and related by ten
scandalised neighbours of
Totnes in 1699

Todd Gray

THE
MINT
PRESS

First published in Great Britain by The Mint Press, 2001

© Todd Gray and The Mint Press 2001

ISBN 1-903356-15-6

Cataloguing in Publication Data
CIP record for this title is available from the British Library

The Mint Press
18 The Mint
Exeter, Devon
England EX4 3BL

Cover design and text design by Delphine Jones

Cover illustration by D. Rogers

Printed and bound in Great Britain
by Short Run Press Ltd, Exeter.

CONTENTS

INTRODUCTION

For three hundred years the Reverend John Prince has been celebrated for his *Danmonii Orientales Ilustres*, more commonly known as *The Worthies of Devon*, a book about the county's most notable individuals which remains a key work on Devon. However, at the time of its publication in 1701 the reputation of Mr Prince was seriously compromised by scandal. Over the centuries historians largely forgot he had been considered notorious amongst his contemporaries. Only a handful archivists charged with looking after a series of depositions which chronicled Mr Prince's curious indiscretion were aware of the details. The immediate consequence of the scandal was Prince being deprived of his living. In 1981 the late Michael Smith raised the issue of the scandal and suggested that Prince's downfall was due to political necessity and questions the reliability of the witnesses.[1] But the full details of the story, as told by those who were personally involved, have remained unknown and unpublished partly because of its bawdy language and fullsome details. It is those ten testimonies which are reproduced in the following pages.[2]

Prince was born in 1643 in Axminster, received his BA from Brasenose College Oxford, in 1664 and after several posts in Devon became Vicar of Totnes in 1675. He remained there for six years until he was instituted to the vicarage of the neighbouring parish of Berry Pomeroy.[3]

On the evening of 24 April 1699 Prince was aged 52 and had been married to his wife Gertrude for some 25 years but was childless.

Mary Southcote, an unmarried woman who also lived in the parish of Berry Pomeroy, was 29 years old.[4] Any details on their relationship prior to that day are unknown but at about eight o'clock that evening they met in Totnes near the Seven Stars. The events after this point become somewhat confused but the testimonies of the ten witnesses appear to agree on the general events.

The two were overheard having a polite conversation in what is now Fore Street before Southcote rode to a bake house and Prince went to an alehouse on Fore Street, a few doors away from the Seven Stars,[5] which was run by one John Angel. The vicar was shown into a private room, given a flagon of ale or cider and then he sent a message, possibly two, with a child to Southcote who was still at the bake house. She was told that Prince desired her to visit him.

Mary Southcote was observed arriving at the alehouse and in the subsequent hour or so at least nine neighbours climbed upon a bench in order to peek through a broken pane of glass at Prince and Southcote. It is surprising that Prince and Southcote were not disturbed by either the number of people clambering to watch or their setting off to find other voyeurs. Their performance was finally interrupted by one observer calling out *'Shame'* through the window.

The following day the news spread through Totnes and the surrounding villages that Reverend Prince had committed a sexual act with Mary Southcote. A short time afterward nine witnesses were questioned as to what they observed. It was not easy to be certain: irrespective of the practicalities of standing on a wooden bench on a slope at night, there was only candlelight in the room and many of the witnesses tried to ascertain what the couple could have achieved in the positions they were seen in. Evidence of Prince's actions had been found on the floor but the salient point was whether Prince and Southcote achieved full intercourse.

The statements were taken by a church court official in order to determine whether Prince should be ejected from Berry Pomeroy church. Questions were asked by the prosecution (the articles) and by the defence (the interrogatories) which tried to discredit the witnesses with accusations of having bias, using bad language, thieving, being opportunists, committing adultery and being corruptible because of poverty. But the affirmation of two sound witnesses resulted in the removal of Prince from his living. The story did not end there: a year later further evidence questioned the validity of the earlier testimonies and Prince was, a short while later, allowed back into his church.

Prince won his case through a legal technicality. Clearly Prince was engaging in acts which were considered indecent for a married cleric. A witness claimed that Prince told

Southcote's father he had only fondled Mary and that, as far as he knew, she was still a virgin. She stated they did not have intercourse although Prince tried his hardest. His behaviour was clearly not exemplary but how far did they go? The collapse of the case came with the questioning of Walter Bogan's statement, a man who subsequently received a less than flattering portrayal by Prince in his *Worthies of Devon*.[6] Bogan supposedly admitted to a third party that he was not convinced that sexual intercourse had taken place and the testimonies of those who swore to it were discounted because they were too poor to be considered reliable witnesses.

Prince was clearly suspicious that either Bishop Trelawny or his officials were behind the prosecution: one defence question implies that the witnesses were cajoled by John Atherton who organised the testimonies on behalf of the diocese. The suggestion has also been made that Sir Edward Seymour, who was patron of the living and a prominent politician at Westminster, was uncomfortable with having a scandalous cleric in his own parish. It may have been that Prince was the victim of a local conspiracy.

There are some problems with the documents: the first two pages were later badly damaged and not all the words have survived. There are words with archaic meanings which makes understanding the sense difficult. Among these are quarrel (a diamond-shaped pane of glass), ceiling (panelling, tapestry screen or curtain), form (a wooden seat without a back), fye (an indignant exclamation), one half parts (a portion), trembling (apprehensive), naught (wicked), boggled (hesitant) and incontinence (not being chaste).

Nevertheless, in spite of the problems the statements make fascinating reading. They reveal the insular nature of the small market town and each witness provides slightly different details which alter the reader's understanding of the night's events. The only reasonable way of deciding what happened that night is by carefully examining all the testimonies of what was a very curious incident in the history of Totnes.

[1] Michael Smith, 'John Prince and the publication of The Worthies of Devon', *Devon & Cornwall Notes & Queries*, 34 (1981), 301-7.
[2] Devon Record Office, CC178/Berry Pomeroy 1.
[3] I am grateful to Ian Maxted for supplying me with details of Prince from his forthcoming entry in the Dictionary of National Biography.
[4] Mary Southcote was baptised in Berry Pomeroy on 18 January 1670.
[5] The Seven Stars had been built nineteen years earlier in 1680: I am grateful to Jill Drysdale for this information.
[6] Smith, 'John Prince', 302.

I would like to thank John Draisey, Sue Laithwaite and Margery Rowe for their help and advice. Mr. D Rogers kindly supplied the cover illustration.

At Totnes
1 August 1699

Walter Bogan
of Gatcombe, gentleman, 36 years old.

To the first article, he answers that the articulate Mr John Prince hath been reputed a Priest in Holy Orders and Vicar of the parish of Berry Pomeroy in the articles mentioned for the space of fifteen or twenty years last past or thereabouts.

To the third article, he answers that upon or about the fourth and twentieth day of April last as this deponent being at the house of one William Payne at the sign of the Seven Stars in the town of Totnes in the county of Devon about eight or nine the clock in the evening, and being about to leave the said house to go home, one John Tucker of the said town of Totnes (a witness sworn in this cause) came to the deponent saying *'Master will you see a show?'*

Whereto this deponent replied that he could not… for he was going home but the said Tucker was very eager… and thereupon this deponent asked him [what] it was, to which the said Tucker replied *'that Parson Prince was fucking a woman at Angel's house like mad'*, upon which this deponent went to the said Angel's door, being two or three doors distant from the said Payne's house, and stepped upon a bench or seat of the porch before the door of the said Angel's house and looked in at a window of a little parlour of the said house towards the street, there being a whole quarrel of the glass broken.

And there this deponent saw the said Prince with his back towards the wall resting on a bench and a woman up against him with his hands clasped round her breech or buttocks under her coats as he supposed. And the Motions of their bodies towards each other and this deponent heard the said woman say *'Oh, sir, you'll do me harm'* whereto Mr Prince replied saying *'No love, I'll do thee no harm'* and bid her bear up her body a little more and then said *'Now twill do'* and then would be silent a little time.

And whilst they were so, this deponent would observe the motion of their bodies to each other and this deponent believes he continued looking on them about a quarter of an hour and they never parted from that posture all that time, and at that posture this deponent left them, there being divers other people in the street in the said Angel's door discoursing about it before being together in that room.

And whilst they were so together this deponent heard the said Mr Prince bid the said woman to come next morning early at his house whereto she replied that she had no pretence or errand there, to which he replied make any pretence or errand for I'll be first that shall be stirring... Nicholas Gay being come to the said door… cried out saying *'Fye, for shame, for shame'*. Some people about the doors broke in upon them and this deponent went away. But this deponent did not know the woman but the people then about the door said it was Mary Southcote, Thomas Southcote's daughter. And this deponent supposeth from what he saw and observed that the said Mr Prince and the woman had or endeavoured the Carnal Knowledge of each other's body.

To the fourth article, he answers that since the premise there hath been and is a public report within the town of Totnes aforesaid and Berry Pomeroy and parishes adjoining that the said Mr Prince and Mary Southcote had been naught [wicked] together and lain with each other at the said Angel's house aforesaid at the time deposed.

•

To the first interrogatory, he answers that he came hither to give his evidence in this cause upon a letter from his fellow witness Mr John Atherton who wrote this respondent that he had received a decree from the court against him to that purpose and that if he did not now appear he would be summoned to appear at Exeter.

To the third interrogatory, he answers that his fellow witness John Tucker is a common bailiff.

To the sixth interrogatory, he answers that at the time aforesaid when this respondent so looked in at the window aforesaid he saw many people thereabout the door and window of the said Angel's house, amongst whom were his fellow witnesses John Tucker, Nicholas Gay, Edward Rounsevall, William Payne, and Elizabeth Payne his wife and several others, who came and went off again and whom he cannot recollect.

To the seventh interrogatory, he answers that the actions this respondent observed between Mr Prince and the woman aforesaid was about eight or nine of the clock in the evening. And this respondent saw through a broken quarrel as before deposed, there being a candle in the room.

To the tenth interrogatory, he answers that he doth not remember that ever he declared to any person that he had seen nothing of indecency by Mr Prince or knew no hurt by him.

SECOND WITNESS
John Tucker
of Totnes in the county of Devon, dyer, 28 years old.

To the first article, he answers that Mr John
Prince in the articles named hath been generally
reputed a Priest in Holy Orders and Vicar of the
parish of Berry Pomeroy for several years last
past.

To the third article, he answers that upon or
about the four and twentieth day of April last past
about eight or nine of the clock in the evening
this deponent going to the house of one John
Angel, a public inn in the town of Totnes, to
enquire for the said Angel, his wife told him he
was gone to bed but this deponent not believing
her and seeing a light in the parlour of the house

and supposing the said Angel might be there, he opened the said parlour door and looking into the room, he saw a woman there who stepped at the table and turned her back to this deponent and a man slipped behind the door upon which this deponent pulled fast the door again.

And then this deponent going out at the door saw William Payne, William Hoyle and William Amyott looking in at a window of the said parlour upon which this deponent asked them what they meant by looking in at people's windows after that manner, then the said Hoyle and Amyott bid this deponent be quiet and he should have half parts, then this deponent asked them what they meant by half parts, then they bid this deponent look in at the window, then this deponent stepped up on a bench or seat in a porch at the said Angel's door and looked in at the said barton window through a quarrel of glass broken (there being a candle burning on the table). And there saw the aforesaid Mr Prince with his back against the wall sitting or resting himself on a bench in the room. And Mary Southcote in the articles named close up against him with her coats up before, so that this deponent saw her thigh that was towards this deponent and his hands clasped about her breech or buttocks, and this deponent observed the motions of their bodies towards each other, and the said woman's hands, being against the said wall the said Mr Prince bid her take off her hands from the wall and stand upright and accordingly she did take off her hands from the said wall (then this deponent admiring at it and saying he could never have believed such a thing if he had not seen it with his eyes). Then the said Hoyles and Amyott said that he had fucked her twice already, then this deponent went at the house of his fellow witness William Payne about two or three doors distant from the said Angel's house and acquainted his fellow witness Walter Bogan esquire what he had seen between the said Mr

Prince and Mary Southcote and thereupon the said Mr Bogan went down with this deponent at the said Angel's door and then the said Mr Bogan looked in at the said window for a considerable time and one Edward Rounsevall also looked in at the said window.

The said Rounsevall afterwards said if an Angel had come from heaven and told him so, he should not have believed it, if he had not seen it with his own eyes, meaning the actions between Mr Prince and Mary Southcott. Then one Mr Nicholas Gay came there likewise and looked in at the said window and cried out *fye, fye, shame. You deserve to be hanged'* or to that purpose,

Then the said Mr Gay and this deponent went to the parlour door and opened it and this deponent went into the room and the said Mary Southcote then slunk out of the room and the said Mr Prince stood at the door, then this deponent asked him *'whether he were not ashamed of these things?'* or to that effect to which the said Mr Prince replied *'of what should I be ashamed of?'*

And then this deponent took up his ring which he said had dropped off his finger, then this deponent took up the candle and took up the ring which lay on the ground and then this deponent observed some seed of the said Mr Prince's spilt on the ground (as he conceived it to be) and then again asked Mr Prince what he had done, *or I'm ashamed of what you have done, I believe you are not sensible yourself what you have done.* And in a little time this deponent went away leaving the said Mr Prince in the parlour and by the time the said Mary Southcote went off from the said house there were got about the said Angel's door a great number of people. And as this deponent believes, would have used some violence to the said Mary Southcote if this deponent had not prevented them.

And this deponent believes from the postures and actions which he saw and observed between the said Mr Prince and Mary Southcote that they had or endeavoured to have the Carnal Knowledge of each other's body. And the said Mr Prince, whilst this deponent was at the window, appointed the said Mary Southcote to meet him next morning early at his house & he would be the first stirring and she should know by his putting some straw at the door.

To the fourth article, he answers that since the premises there has been and is a public fame and report within the town of Totnes and parish of Berry Pomeroy and parishes adjoining that the said Mr Prince and Mary Southcote were guilty of Adultery or Incontinency together at the said Angel's house at the time aforesaid.

●

To the first interrogatory, he answers that he hath come hither to give his evidence in this cause being summoned by process of the court and expects to be paid for his loss of time in giving his evidence by the prosecutor within this cause but hath not received nor been promised to receive any other reward.

To the second interrogatory, he answers that he hath not been taught or instructed by any person what or how to say or depose in this cause nor is he to have any benefit or advantage by the success of this suit and is worth above five hundred pounds [if] his debts [owing to him were] paid.

To the sixth interrogatory, he answers that there were present at the time aforesaid whilst the said Mr Prince and Mary Southcote were in the said Angel's chamber, his fellow witnesses Walter Bogan esquire, Edward Rounsevall, Nicholas Gay, William Payne and Elizabeth his wife, William Hoyle, William Amyott, and several other people were gathered together about the said Angel's house a little before the said Mary Southcote went away from the said house.

To the eighth interrogatory, he answers that when this respondent went first to the said

Angel's house and there saw Mr Prince and Mary Southcote as before deposed, the said Hoyles and Amyott said to this respondent that he should have half parts. And believes they did not disturb the said Mr Prince and Mary Southcote because they had some design of making a prey upon the said Mr Prince. And is induced so to believe because they said to this respondent he should have half parts but this respondent refused to be concerned with them.

To the ninth interrogatory, he answers that Mr John Willing in the interrogatory named is this respondent's father-in-law but this respondent does not believe he is an enemy to Mr Prince in this suit nor never heard him to speak ill of him or to say he would give a sum of money to have him turned out of his place or any thing to that purpose.

To the thirteenth interrogatory, he answers that William Hoyles and William Amyott in the interrogatories named are poor people of little or no reputation and this respondent believes they never receive the sacrament.

To the fourteenth interrogatory, he answers that near about a quarter of a year since Mr John Atherton, register of the archdeaconry of Totnes, sent for this respondent to come unto him at his house in Totnes and accordingly this respondent went unto him. When he came the said Mr Atherton told this respondent that he had received a letter from Exeter by order of my Lord Bishop to give an account how the matter stood about the report between the said miscreant Mr Prince and Mary Southcote. And desired this respondent to relate unto him what he knew or to that effect. And thereupon this respondent related unto him of what he knew of the matter which was to the effect of his fellow witnesses' depositions but this respondent was not threatened or persuaded by the said Mr Atherton or any other person to say anything more than what he really knew and saw, but only to give an impartial account of what he knew and had seen.

To the additional article, he answers that the said Mr Prince at present is and hath been for several years last past a married man having a very sober and virtue woman to his wife of good quality and connection and so generally reputed in the town of Totnes and parish of Berry Pomeroy and country near about.

Nicholas Gay

of Totnes in the county of Devon, baker, 28 years old.

To the first article, he answers that Mr John Prince in the articles named at present is and for several years last past hath been generally reputed and accounted a priest in holy orders and vicar of the parish of Berry Pomeroy.

To the third article, he answers that upon or about the four and twentieth day of April last past this deponent and his previous fellow witnesses Walter Bogan esquire and one Mr Edward Symons and his fellow witness Edward Rounsevall being together at the house of one William Payne, a public beer house in Totnes aforesaid, about eight or nine of the clock in the evening, his fellow witness John Tucker came into the room where they were and under a seeming concern, said to them that Mr Prince was lying, or used some such word, with Thomas Southcote's daughter at John Angel's house, and that he trembled to see what he had seen between them, and then desired the company to go and see them, which they at first seemed unwilling to do.

But the said John Tucker being very earnest with them Mr Bogan and the said Edward Rounsevall went from this deponent and the said Mr Symon's company to the said Angel's house. And in some short time after the said Rounsevall came back again to this deponent and the said Mr Symons, then they asked him how he found it, to which the said Rounsevall replied it was the horrendous thing that ever he saw.

Then this deponent in a little time went also down to the said Angel's house (being a public ale house about three or four doors distant from

the said Payne's house), and there found many
people gathered together about the door and
some person or persons standing up on a bench
in the porch of the said house looking in through
a broken quarrel of glass into the parlour
window. And then this deponent stepped up on
the said bench and also looked into the said
window through a broken glass and there saw
the said Mr Prince sitting on a bench or form
against the wall or ceiling of the room. And the
articulate Mary Southcote standing between his
legs with her hands upon his shoulders or upon
his neck but where his hands were he doth not
remember he saw, but being under a great
surprise to hear what he heard John Tucker and
Edward Rounsevall to say and seeing them in this
indecent posture, this deponent immediately
cried out, '*Fye, fye for shame, tis a shame for a
man of your coat* [i.e. cloth] *to do this*' or used
words to the like effect.

And then the said John Tucker and this

deponent went into the entry of the said house and the said Tucker opened the said parlour door and the said Tucker went into the parlour and this deponent stood at the door, then the said Tucker asked Mr Prince whether he were not ashamed of what he had done, whereto Mr Prince replied *'Why? What have I done?'*. Then Tucker taking the candle that was in the room in his hand and stooping towards the ground said *'I think you don't know what you have done. Look here you may see what you have done'* and then this deponent and the said Tucker came away leaving the said Mr Prince in the said parlour, but the said Mary Southcote came out of the room and went away upon this deponent calling into them through the glass. And as she came out of the house and went [into] the street, the people shouted at her calling her *'drunken whore'* and the like.

But this deponent doth not believe that at that instant of time when this deponent looked through the glass as aforesaid the said Mr Prince and Mary Southcott were in the Act of Uncleanness, this deponent not observing any of her clothes up or any other action to induce him so to believe but what passed between them before this deponent came he knoweth not.

To the fourth article, he answers that since the premise there hath been a general and public report within the town of Totnes aforesaid that the said Mr Prince and Mary Southcote were guilty of adultery or incontinency with each other at the time aforesaid and this deponent sayeth that the next Saturday after the premise the said Mary Southcote coming to Totnes Market, this deponent was informed that abundance of people of the town and country were gathered together about her and would have been very rude with her and abused her if she had not been taken care of and protected by William Taylor, a constable of Totnes aforesaid, and so much the said constable told this deponent.

To the additional article, he answers that the said Mr Prince at present is and for several years last hath been a married man and his wife is generally reputed to be a very good and virtuous woman.

•

To the first interrogatory, he answers that his fellow witness John Tucker is a common bailiff and is pretty much addicted to common swearing.

To the second interrogatory, he answers that he hath heard that the said John Tucker was about two months, or a quarter of a year since, in a furse [gorse] house with a woman and that his wife came there and found them together, but whether she found them in any evil act this respondent hath not heard. But some people have from their being there together, inferred that they were naught together.

To the fifth interrogatory, he answers that shortly after midsummer last past this respondent being at the house of one Richard Blackbourne, an innkeeper in Totnes, in the next room there were the said John Tucker and Mr Trust and one Hutchens in the interrogatory named, and they were then discoursing of a difference that had happened between the said Hutchins and Tucker on the road coming from Newton Fair or Market and the said Tucker said that Hutchens struck him and he struck Hutchens but he did not design to do him any injury, then said Mr Trust '*my man* (meaning the said Hutchens being his servant) *sold bullocks at the fair and received money but hath not yet given it me*' or '*I don't know what's become of it*', but this respondent thinks the matter was then composed between them for that he never heard any more of it since.

To the ninth interrogatory, he answers that Mr John Willing in the interrogatories named is father-in-law to the aforesaid John Tucker but doth not know or believe that the said Mr Willing is an enemy to Mr Prince nor never heard Mr Willing to say that he would give a sum of money to turn Mr Prince out of his benefice nor any discourse to that purpose.

To the thirteenth interrogatory, he answers that the said William Amyott and William Hoyles are poor people and he believes they seldom or never received the sacrament but hath heard no other ill of them.

To the fourteenth interrogatory, he answers that he had not been persuaded or threatened to give his evidence in this cause by any person whatsoever but came to give his evidence herein being summoned by processes out of this court.

To the fifteenth interrogatory, he answers that he this deponent was one of the last that went to the said Angel's house and saw Mr Prince and Mary Southcote there as aforesaid deposed. And as soon as he saw them he cried *'Fye, for shame'* to them as before he hath deposed, but believes they were there some considerable time before this respondent went there, it being (as this respondent believes) above half an hour from the time the said John Tucker came to the said Payne's house and acquainted this respondent and the said Mr Bogan, Mr Symons, and Mr Rounsevall of it and the time that this respondent went thither. And when this respondent saw them the said Mary Southcote was standing between the said Mr Prince's legs with her hand on his shoulder or about his neck, he sitting on a bench or form against the wall or ceiling of the room as this deponent hath before deposed. And this respondent cannot believe or guess from the posture he saw them in that they were then committing the Act of Adultery.

FOURTH WITNESS
William Amyott
of Totnes in the county of Devon, cordwainer, 50 years old.

To the first article, he answers that the articulate Mr John Prince at present is and for several years last past hath been generally reputed a Priest in Holy Orders and Vicar of the parish of Berry Pomeroy.

To the third article, he answers that sometime in the month of April last past (as near as this deponent can recollect the time) this deponent being in his own house in Totnes aforesaid, about eight or nine of the clock in the evening, one William Hoyle alias Gyles came to this deponent in seeming haste and took this deponent by the sleeve saying *'come away along with me, it may be worth us five pounds'*.

And was very earnest with him to go, and thereupon this deponent supposing it had been to assist in the arresting some person (he this deponent sometime executing warrants as a bailiff) went with the said Hoyles and he carried this deponent at the door of one John Angell's house, a public inn or alehouse in Totnes aforesaid, and then the said Hoyles stepped up on a bench or seat in a porch before the door of the said Angell's house and looked in at a parlour window of the said Angell's house, there being a quarrel broken out, and bid this deponent step up on the said bench and look in likewise.

And accordingly this deponent did step up on the said bench or seat and they both looked in at the said window and, there being a candle on the table in the said room burning, this deponent there saw the aforesaid Mr Prince sitting or resting himself on a bench or form against the wall or ceiling in the said parlour and Mary Southcote in the articles named standing up against him with one of her arms about his neck or his shoulders, bearing in her body towards him, and this deponent observed her coats to be a little up and saw something white but whether it was her thigh or her shift or Mr Prince's hand he cannot take upon him to say. And this deponent remembers he heard Mr Prince to say to her (having his hand and arm about her upon her clothes) that he would do her no harm.

But this deponent believes that in the posture he saw the said Mr Prince and Mary Southcote they could not commit the act of adultery though their posture and actions were very indecent and uncomely. But in some short time after this deponent had looked into the window as aforesaid, there came his previous fellow witnesses Walter Bogan esquire, John Tucker, Edward Rounsevall, Nicholas Gay and William Payne and several others and looked into the window. And then this deponent could see no more at the window.

And in some short time afterwards the said John Tucker opened the said door and went into the said parlour, the said Nicholas Gay standing at the said door, and there was some discourse passed between the said Mr Prince and John Tucker but what the said discourse was he cannot remember but observed the said Tucker to take up the said Mr Prince's ring from the ground, this deponent being then in the same room but as soon as the door was opened, the said Mary Southcote went out of the room. And in a little time after the said Nicholas Gay and John Tucker went away and left the said Mr Prince in the said room.

And the next morning the said Mr Prince came again into the town of Totnes and went into the said Angel's house and this deponent and the said William Hoyle standing in the street of Totnes and seeing the said Mr Prince go into the said Angel's house they went in after him. And then Mr Prince spake to this deponent, and the said Hoyle, saying *'Gentlemen, I hope you see no hurt last night and that you won't endeavour to take away my Auditory'* and then called for a flagon of cider and made them drink and gave them six pence a piece and so they went away.

To the fourth article, he answers that since the premise there hath been a public discourse in the town of Totnes and parish of Berry Pomeroy and parishes adjacent that the said Mr Prince and the said Mary Southcote had been guilty of Adultery or Incontinency together at the said Angel's house at the time aforesaid.

To the additional article, he answers that the said Mr Prince at present is and for several years last past hath been a married man, and his wife is a woman of a good character being generally accounted a very virtuous good woman and this deponent never heard any ill of Mr Prince until the time aforesaid at the said Angel's house.

•

To the third interrogatory, he answers that John Tucker in the interrogatories named is a common bailiff and much addicted to common swearing and a person of little reputation and with whom persons don't care to have to do.

To the fourth interrogatory, he answers that he hath heard that the said John Tucker was lately found with a woman not his own wife but how, where, or after what manner they were found he did not hear.

To the fifth interrogatory, he answers that he hath heard that the said John Tucker and one Hutchens (in the interrogatories named) had lately some difference on the road but how it happened or upon what occasion it was this respondent did not hear but that the said Tucker had done amiss on the road.

To the sixth interrogatory, he answers that Mr Willing in the interrogatory named is father-in-law to the said John Tucker, but is not (as he believes) an enemy to Mr Prince nor did this respondent ever hear that Mr Willing should declare that he would give a sum of money to turn Mr Prince out of his benefice or anything to that purpose.

To the fifteenth interrogatory, he answers that after this respondent first went to the said Angel's door with the said Hoyle as aforesaid, he continued there about the door until the said Mary Southcote went away. But after the said John Tucker, Mr Bogan and the rest of the company came this respondent did not look into the window.

Edward Rounsevall

of Littlehempston in the county of Devon, yeoman,
60 years old.

To the first article, he answers that the articulate
Mr Prince at present is and for many years last
past hath been generally reputed a Priest in Holy
Orders and Vicar of the parish of Berry Pomeroy.

To the third article, he answers that upon or
about the three or four and twentieth day of April
last past this deponent being at the house of one
William Payne, a public ale house in Totnes, with
his previous fellow witnesses Walter Bogan
esquire and Nicholas Gay about eight or nine of
the clock that evening his previous fellow witness
John Tucker came to the said Payne's house and
told the said Mr Bogan, Nicholas Gay and this

deponent that the said Mr Prince was lying (or some such word) with a girl at John Angel's house, and was earnest with the said Mr Bogan to go and see them but the said Mr Bogan was at first very unwilling, but the said John Tucker being very earnest with him, he at length was persuaded to go and this deponent went with him and when they came at the said Angel's door, the said Mr Bogan stepped up on a bench in the porch at the said and looked into the parlour of the said house through the window, the glass being broken.

And after the said Mr Bogan had looked in sometime he stepped down from the bench again and then this deponent stepped up on the said bench and looked into the said window. And there saw Mr Prince sitting on a bench or form against the partition or wall of the said room and a woman standing very close to him between his legs and her hands or arms upon his shoulder which this deponent seeing, he presently stepped down again from the said bench. And speaking to the company then gathered about the door, said *'Fye upon it, let some body go into the room and speak to them'*. And so this deponent went back again to the said Payne's house, leaving the said Mr Bogan and John Tucker and several other people about the said door and window.

But this deponent did not observe the said woman's clothes or coats to be taken up nor did he see where the said Mr Prince's hands were, nor did he hear any discourse between them, he looking a very little while into the window and presently stepping down the bench again and going away. But this deponent believes that in the posture he then saw the said Mr Prince and the said woman it was not possible for him to enter the body of the said woman or to commit the Act of Adultery with her.

To the fourth article, he answers that since the time aforesaid, there hath been a public fame and report within the town of Totnes and parish of Berry Pomeroy and parishes adjacent that the said Mr Prince and one Mary Southcote (being the woman said to be called by that name which this deponent saw with the said Mr Prince in the said Angel's house at the time aforesaid) had been guilty of adultery or laying together at the said Angel's house at the time before deposed.

To the additional article, he answers that the said Mr Prince at present is and for many years last past hath been a married man. And his wife hath the general character of a very good and virtuous woman. And very civil and obliging and this deponent believes the character of her to be true, he knowing her very well.

•

To the third interrogatory, he answers that John Tucker named is a common bailiff and addicted to common swearing and sometimes this respondent hath seen him distempered with drink, but at the time when the said Mr Prince and Mary Southcote were at Angel's house as aforesaid the said Tucker was very sober.

To the fourth interrogatory, he answers that he hath heard that the said John Tucker was taken with another woman by his wife but at what place or in what manner he was taken or whether in doing any evil act with her he did not hear.

To the fifth interrogatory, he answers that he hath heard there happened some difference lately on the road between the said John Tucker and one Hutchens in the said interrogatories named, and that there upon the said Hutchens being afraid of him left his horse on the road and went away from him another way but what was the occasion of the said difference between them this respondent knoweth not.

To the eighth interrogatory, he answers that he knows William Hoyles alias Gyles in the interrogatories named, who lived a servant with this respondent for several months about six years since and during his living with this respondent behaved himself very well, and this respondent never heard any hurt of him since.

To the fifteenth interrogatory, he answers that when this respondent saw the said Mr Prince and the woman aforesaid (whose name he hath since understood to be Mary Southcote) she was standing between his legs as before deposed.

William Hoyle

of Totnes in the county of Devon, clothier, 40 years old.

To the first article, he answers that about three or four months since (as near as this deponent can report the time) he being sitting at the door of one John Angel's, a public alehouse in Totnes aforesaid, about eight of the clock in the evening he saw the articulate Mr John Prince to come down the street of Totnes. And as he came near the said Angel's door he met Mary Southcote in the articles named in the public street. And then spake to her and took her by the hand and saluted her and asked her how merry they were at Woody Inn (being a house by the Water Side about half a mile from Totnes where people usually go to make merry) to which she replied they were very merry, then Mr Prince asked her where she was going, to which she replied she was going to the bake house, then Mr Prince asked her how long she would stay there and she answered about half an hour, and then the said Mr Prince and Mary Southcote parted. Mr Prince going one way towards his home and the said Mary Southcote another way towards the bake house.

But in a very little time the said Mr Prince came back again and went into the said Angel's house and asked for a room to drink a flagon of beer or cider, and then showed him into a little room called the Parlour. And he having been there a little time he sent a little girl of the said Angel's house to call the said Mary Southcote. And in some short time about a quarter of an hour as he guesses, the said Mary Southcote came and went into the room where the said Mr Prince was.

And this deponent seeing the said Mary Southcote go into that room, he being sitting on the bench in the porch before the said door, stepped up on the bench and looked into the said parlour window which is adjoining to the said porch there being a quarrel of glass broken. And then this deponent saw the said Mary Southcote as soon as she came into the room to take the said Mr Prince about the neck and kiss him. And the said Mr Prince kissed her again and then in a very little time Mr Prince sat down on a bench or form in the said Room. And the said Mary Southcote sat down upon one of his knees and put her arm about his neck, then this deponent went away and called his previous fellow witness William Amyott from his house, a little distant from the said Amyott's house to come along with him telling the said Amyott it might be something in his way or to that effect. And thereupon the said Amyott came with this deponent to the said Angel's door. And this deponent bid the said Amyott look in at the said parlour window which accordingly he did by stepping up on the bench aforesaid, and in a little time came down again.

And very shortly after his previous fellow witness John Tucker came to the said Angel's door, and having (as this deponent believes) seen the said Amyott looking in at the said window, he the said Tucker looked in likewise. And after a little time went from thence to the house of one William Payne about three or four doors distant from the said Angel's, and in a short time returned again. And as this defendant was told (he being gone into the kitchen of the said Angel's house) there came with him or a little after him his previous fellow witnesses Walter Bogan esquire, Edward Rounsevall and Nicholas Gay. And then there was a noise in the street and several people gathered together about the said Angel's door. And in some short time some of the company opened the said parlour door and went into the room where the said Mr Prince and Mary Southcote were. And thereupon in a little time they both went away.

And the next morning the said Mr Prince came again to the said Angel's house. And this deponent and the said William Amyott being in the street a little distant from the said Angel's door and seeing the said Mr Prince go into the said Angel's house, they went in after him. And then he called for a flagon of ale or cider and made them drink. And said to them *'Gentlemen, I hope you saw no hurt by me last night'* or to that effect. And gave them six pence a piece to drink his health and so they went away.

To the fourth article, he answers that since the premise there hath been a public report in the town of Totnes that the said Mr Prince and Mary Southcote had been naught together at the said Angel's house at the time aforesaid.

•

To the first interrogatory, he answers that he came hither to be a witness in this cause, being warned by a process out of this court but that he hath not received or been promised any thing for giving his testimony in this cause but expects to be paid for his loss of time.

To the second interrogatory, he answers that he hath not been taught or instructed by any person what or how to depose in this cause nor is he to reap any benefit or advantage by the success thereof. And sayeth he is a poor man and lives by his labour and is worth little or nothing.

To the third interrogatory, he answers that his previous fellow witness John Tucker is a common bailiff, much addicted to common swearing and is quarrelsome in his drink, and believes he is a person unto whose sayings or swearing there is little credit to be given.

To the fourth interrogatory, he answers that he hath heard some people lately to say that John Tucker was catched with a woman on a furse faggot but whether he were so catched by his wife or not he did not hear nor what they were doing of.

To the sixth interrogatory, he answers that when he saw Mr Prince go into Angel's house as before he hath deposed he this respondent was sent for to come at the said Angel's house to look after the said Angel's horse, he being then come home from a journey. And what he saw as before he hath deposed was by chance and not any design of this respondent's.

To the seventh interrogatory, he answers that he believes it was between eight and nine of the clock when he saw Mr Prince and the said Mary Southcote together as before deposed.

To the eighth interrogatory, he answers that when this deponent called the said Amyott as before he hath deposed, he told the said Amyott to come along with him for that it might be something in his way, or might get money by it, or to that effect. And when he and the said Amyott came they would have gone into the said room where the said Mr Prince and Mary Southcote were, but Mrs Angel, the woman of the house, would not permit them saying How should she be paid her reckoning then?

To the fourteenth interrogatory, he answers that he hath not been persuaded nor threatened to give his evidence in this cause, but came in obedience to the process of this court being summoned thereunto but never was in any garden house with any person about it.

To the fifteenth interrogatory, he answers that this respondent was at the said Angel's when the said Mr Prince first came there and when the said Mary Southcote, and as soon as she went into the parlour he looked into the window and saw them kiss each other and she to sit on his knee as before he hath deposed. And then went and called the said Amyott but this respondent did not afterwards look into the said window, nor did this respondent see any other actions between them. And is assured that whilst he so saw them they were not guilty of adultery or any other indecency than what he hath before expressed.

SEVENTH WITNESS
William Payne
of Totnes in the county of Devon, clothier, 38 years old.

To the first article, he answers that the articulate
Mr Prince hath been for many years last past
generally reputed a Minister in Holy Orders and
Vicar of the parish of Berry Pomeroy.

To the third article, he answers that upon or
about the four and twentieth day of April last past
his previous fellow witnesses Walter Bogan
esquire, Nicholas Gay, Edward Rounsevall and
one Mr Edward Symons being at this deponent's
house in Totnes aforesaid, about nine of the clock
in the evening, his previous fellow witness John
Tucker came to this deponent's house and came
up into the chamber where this deponent and the

said Mr Bogan, Mr Gay, Mr Rounsevall, and Mr Symons were, and being under a seeming great surprise, said that Mr Prince was down at Angel's house knocking, or fucking, Mr Southcote's daughter and that they were at it when he came away and that her coats were up behind, that he could see her breech and would have the company go down and see it.

And a little after, the said Tucker came to this deponent's house his previous fellow witness William Amyott came also to this deponent's house and in this deponent's kitchen told this deponent laughing that if he would see a sight or a show he should go down to Angel's house for Mr Prince and Mr Southcote's daughter were there at it, he never saw the like and that her coats were up thus high pointing with his hands as high as his middle and that he saw her arse several times.

And in a short time the said Mr Bogan and Mr Rounsevall went from this deponent's house to the said Angels (being three or four doors distant from this deponent's house) and having been absent a little time the said Mr Rounsevall returned again, then this deponent asked him how he found it, whereto the said Rounsevall replied that if an Angel had come from heaven and told him such things of Mr Prince he would not believed it, but (said he) *'Now I have seen it with my eyes'*. And about half an hour after the return of the said Rounsevall (as near as he can guess the time), this deponent and the said Mr Gay went down to the said Angel's house and there was Mr Bogan and several other people then gathered together about the said Angel's door shouting and making sports about it, then the said Mr Gay and this deponent stepped up on a bench of a porch at the said Angel's door and looked in at a parlour window of the said Angel's house adjoining to the said porch through a quarrel of glass broken and there this deponent saw the said Mr Prince sitting on a bench or form in the said parlour and Mary Southcote in the articles named standing between his legs with her hands resting against the wall or ceiling of the parlour or on his shoulder.

Then Mr Gay immediately cried *'Fye, fye, for shame'* upon which the said Mary Southcote turned about her head to look towards the window and the said Mr Prince endeavoured to hide his head under her arm or one side of her. And then in a very little time the said Mary Southcote came out of the room and house and went towards her home and as she passed along the street, people followed after her, she having then a horse in her hand which was tied to the said Angel's door whilst she was in the house. And then this deponent came away leaving the said Mr Gay, John Tucker and several other persons about the said Angel's door and the said Mr Prince in the parlour.

And the said Mr Bogan, Mr Gay and John Tucker returned again to this deponent's house and all related what they had seen and heard. And the said Mr Bogan then related what he saw and said that he verily believed from the posture and actions he saw between them that he was fucking of her, though it was hard (as he said) to judge. And the said Tucker also related what he saw and said he saw her thighs several times and did believe from the posture and actions he saw between that he was knocking of her. And said that whilst he was looking into the said parlour he saw the said Mary Southcote come off from the said Mr Prince and went to the table in the room to drink a glass of cider. And then he saw Mr Prince his privates hang out of his breeches.

And also related that after Mr Gay had disturbed them, he went into the parlour and then asked Mr Prince whether he were not ashamed of these things. And that he the said Tucker stooping down to take up Mr Prince's ring for him which was dropped on the ground, he there observed his seed to be dropped on the ground. And said to him, *'Here is enough to frame you'.*

To the additional article, he answers that the said Mr Prince for many years last past hath been and at present is a married man and his wife is generally reputed a very virtuous obliging woman.

●

To the first interrogatory, he answers that he came to give his evidence in this cause being summoned by process out of this court but has not been promised or received nor expects any thing for giving his evidence herein.

To the second interrogatory, he answers that he hath not been taught or instructed by any person how or after what manner to make or frame his deposition in the cause. Nor is he to reap any benefit or advantage by the success or event of this suit. And is worth two hundred pounds [if] his debts [owed to him were] paid.

To the third interrogatory, he answers that his previous fellow witness John Tucker is a hundred bailiff and executes warrants as a common bailiff and is addicted to common swearing. And some people look upon him as a honest fellow and others the contrary, but this respondent never knew any hurt by him.

To the fourth interrogatory, he answers that there was lately a report that the said John Tucker was catched by his wife with a girl but this respondent hath heard his wife to deny any such thing.

To the fifth interrogatory, he answers that there was lately a report that the said John Tucker and one Hutchens, a servant of Mr Trust in the interrogatory named, had a quarrel on the road. And that Tucker should strike him with his whip and thereupon Hutchens rode away from him and went to one Mr Goodridge's house. And left some money that he had at the said Goodridge's house but it was not reported that

Tucker endeavoured to rob him or any thing like it but that the quarrel between them happened about a girl.

To the fourteenth interrogatory, he answers he hath not been persuaded or threatened by any person to give his evidence in this cause but came in obedience to the said process of this court.

To the fifteenth interrogatory, he answers that this respondent only saw the said Mary Southcote stand between the legs of the said Mr Prince as before he hath deposed. And believes whilst this respondent saw them together (which was a very little time), they did not commit the Act of Adultery he not observing her clothes up or any motions tending towards it.

Henry Martyn
of Totnes in the county of Devon, fuller, 29 years old.

To the first article, he answers that the articulate Mr John Prince hath been for several years last past and at present is generally reputed a Minister in Holy Orders and Vicar of the said parish of Berry Pomeroy.

To the third article, he answers that about a quarter of a year since this deponent being a tabler [boarder] at the house of one John Angel in Totnes aforesaid, and being in the kitchen of the said house writing of a letter his fellow witness John Tucker came into the said kitchen and asked for the said John Angel, to whom this deponent replied that he was gone to bed. But the said Tucker said he believed he was not, but was in the parlour.

But this deponent said he was gone to bed. Notwithstanding which, the said Tucker went to the parlour and opened the door and looked in. And then shut the door again and came back to this deponent in the kitchen being near adjoining to the said parlour and said *'Mr Prince was in the parlour and had got a whore with him'*. To which this deponent said he would not believe it and the said Tucker went out of the door.

And then this deponent hearing some people about the door of the said house, went out at the said door and there saw his previous fellow witnesses John Tucker, William Amyott, and William Hoyles standing at the door of the said house. And as he thinks were looking in at the parlour window, then this deponent said to them if they saw any uncivil thing they were damned rogues if they did not disturb them.

And then this deponent went in again to the

said kitchen and as he was returning into the said kitchen he cast his eye and looked in through a quarrel broken in the parlour window and then saw Mr Prince sitting on a bench in the room and Mary Southcote in the articles named standing up close against him and they were kissing. But this deponent did not see or observe any other indecent postures or actions between them, he only casting his eye and not staying above a minute or two, or thereabouts. But sometime after this deponent was returned into the kitchen this deponent heard a noise of several people gathered together in the street about the door but this deponent being then very ill in the gout he went out no more amongst them but in some time some of the people opened the said parlour door and the said Mary Southcote went away.

And a little afterwards the said Mr Prince came into the kitchen where this deponent was and called for his reckoning [bill]. And then said *'This is the first time I ever was in the house and I think it shall be the last for I had never such a trick put upon me before'* and said (to the best of this deponent's remembrance) *'I vow to God I did no more hurt or harm than I do now this present'* or expressed himself to that effect. And so left the said house.

To the additional article, he answers that Mr Prince hath been generally reputed a married man for several years past and his wife hath the general character of a very virtuous good woman.

•

To the first interrogatory, he answers that he came hither to give his evidence in this cause being summoned thereto by process out of this court but hath not received, been promised nor expects any reward for giving his evidence in this cause.

To the second interrogatory, he answers that he hath not been taught or instructed by any person how or what to say in this cause nor is he to reap any advantage by the event or success of this suit. And is worth two hundred pounds [if] his debts [were] paid.

To the third interrogatory, he answers that his fellow witness John Tucker is reputed a common bailiff and is a person of little or no reputation, and a common swearer and liar. And this respondent believes he makes no conscience of an oath in common swearing, he having made several lies upon this respondent and sworn to it when this respondent hath known it to be false. But as to his swearing in judgement, he cannot tell what to think of him.

To the fourth interrogatory, he answers that it was lately reported in the town of Totnes that the said Tucker's wife had catched him with another woman in a suspicious place but who the woman was he cannot tell.

To the fifth interrogatory, he answers that there was lately a report in the town of Totnes that there happened a quarrel on the road between the said Tucker and one Hutchens, a servant to one Mr Trust in the said interrogatory named, and that thereupon the said Hutchens left his horse and went away on the road, leaving his horse behind him, and it was said the said Hutchens was afraid of his life, or of his purse, of the said Tucker.

To the fourteenth interrogatory, he answers that he hath not been persuaded or threatened by any person to give his evidence in this cause.

To the fifteenth interrogatory, he answers that when this respondent saw the said Mr Prince and Mary Southcote as aforesaid they were not committing the sin of Adultery as he believes, and in the posture he saw them he believes they could not be guilty of the act he not seeing any of her clothes up and standing upright against him and he sitting on the bench.

John Atherton
of Totnes in the county of Devon, Notary de public,
41 years old.

To the first article, he answers that the articulate Mr Prince hath been for several years last past and at present is a Minister in Holy Orders, and Vicar of the parish of Berry Pomeroy and so generally accounted and reputed.

To the third article he answers, that about the latter end of April last past here was a great noise and general report within the town of Totnes and parishes adjacent that the articulate Mr Prince and Mary Southcote in the articles named had been seen by several persons committing the act of adultery together in the house of one John Angel, a public alehouse in the said town of Totnes, and some few days after, vis-à-vis about the beginning of the month of May last past, this deponent received a letter from Mr Francis Oliver, Deputy Register of the Consistory Court of Exeter, acquainting this deponent that there was a scandalous report about Exeter as if Mr Prince of Berry Pomeroy should be taken with a woman in the act of uncleanness or to that effect.

And therefore, willed this deponent to enquire the truth of the said report as much as he could and give him an account thereof because my Lord Bishop would be satisfied about it, or to that effect. And upon his receipt of the said letter, this deponent sent for the said Mary Southcote to come unto him at his house and accordingly the said Mary Southcote came unto this deponent at his house, there being with her a person whom this deponent thinks she called Brother and then this deponent took her into his office and enquired of her about the said report between her and the said Mr Prince.

And the said Mary Southcott then confessed to this deponent that on the four and twentieth day of April then past about eight of the clock in the afternoon she coming into the town of Totnes on business for her father, met the said Mr Prince at her entrance into the town. And who then saluted her in the street and after asking her some few questions about her father, he parted from her. And she went to the bakehouse and in some short time after she came to the said bakehouse a servant girl belonging to one John Angel (who keeps a public alehouse in Totnes) came to her and acquainted her that Mr Prince was at the said Angel's house and desired to speak with her, and she not going presently, he sent a second time unto her pressing her to make haste to come unto him.

And thereupon she went unto him at the said Angel's house where she found the said Mr

Prince in a parlour or under room of the said House next adjoining to the street where after some discourse had passed between them, the said Mr Prince offered some indecencies and incivilities towards her holding both her hands with one of his hands and putting his other hand under her coats. And after that took out his privy parts and put it into her hand and used several other ill actions with her for the space of about an hour. But denied that he had actually the knowledge of her body after any other manner than by feeling of her with his hand, but said that she believed had she been as willing as Mr Prince, he would have lain with her.

To the fourth article, he answers that some short time after it was reported that the said Mr Prince and Mary Southcote were seen at the said Angel's house as before deposed, the Reverend Mr George Snell, Archdeacon of Totnes, kept his visitation. And at the visitation the Churchwardens of the parish of Berry Pomeroy (where the said Mr

Prince is minister and where the said Mary Southcote lives) exhibited a presentment on their oaths wherein they presented the said Mr Prince, vicar of their said parish, and the said Mary Southcote for lying under a public fame of incontinence being the presentment annexed to the articles in this cause exhibited and on which he is now examined subscribed by Edward Skynner and Robert Tully, who were the churchwardens of the said parish for the last year, this deponent being Register of the said Archdeaconry and present when the said presentment was exhibited.

To the additional article, he answers that the said Mr Prince at present is and for several years last past hath been generally reputed a married man and his wife hath the general character of a very virtuous sober good woman.

•

To the third interrogatory, he answers that John Tucker in the interrogatory named is a common bailiff and was for some years since reputed a loose fellow but for a year or two last past he is said to be much reclaimed.

To the eleventh interrogatory, he answers that the said churchwardens aforesaid at Berry Pomeroy at the visitation held at Totnes on or about the third day of May last past did much scruple the presenting the said Mr Prince and Mary Southcote alleging that they knew nothing of the fact only of the report thereof. And thereupon this respondent told them if they were satisfied there was a public report they ought to present it, and that he conceived they were obliged so to do. Then they acknowledged there was a public fame of the said Mr Prince and Mary Southcote being guilty of incontinence together but insisted that [as] they knowing nothing of the fact were not obliged to present it.

And thereupon they went off from this respondent without giving their presentment and about two hours afterwards this respondent, being in company with the mayor of Totnes and

Counsellor Gibbons, Deputy Recorder of the town and some other persons, the said churchwardens came again into the room where this respondent was with the said Company and desired that they might have some time allowed for the giving their presentment to which this respondent replied that he could not give them a longer time but it must be granted them by the Archdeacon or his Surrogate, then Mr Gibbons asked whether these were the churchwardens of Berry Pomeroy and being told they were, he told them that they ought to present the said Mr Prince and Mary Southcote upon the fame or report that was against them and were obliged to do it by the law, and that if they did not they might be prosecuted for not doing thereof and paid them consider of it and go home and lay their heads to the pillow.

And thereupon the said Churchwardens went away for that night. And the next morning they came again before the said Archdeacon and this respondent and gave in the presentment aforesaid. But this respondent believes they would not have presented the said Mr Prince and Mary Southcote had not this respondent and the said Mr Gibbons discoursed to them in manner as aforesaid for that they offered to exhibit a presentment without mentioning any thing concerning them.

To the twelfth interrogatory, he answers that when the said Mary Southcote came to this respondent at his house, as before deposed, she at first seemed very shy and boggled [hesitant] to say anything of the matter, then this respondent told her she would be obliged to make an answer to the charge against her. And that if she made a fair confession she might fare the better for it or to that effect, but not in the least threatened her, and strictly charged her to be sure not in the least to charge any thing upon Mr Prince but the very truth. And then the said Mary Southcote made the confession to this respondent as before he hath deposed, and after she had made the confession as aforesaid this respondent thinks he told her that if the report between the said Mr Prince and she were proved, she might be enjoined [imposed] penance in three parish churches, but whether he told her so upon her asking him what punishment he thought might be inflicted on her or not he doth not remember.

To the fourteenth interrogatory, he answers that upon receiving the letter from Mr Oliver mentioned in his fellow witness' deposition, this respondent did send for his fellow witness John Tucker (who was generally reported to have seen what passed between the said Mr Prince and Mary Southcote at Angel's house aforesaid).

And the said Tucker came to this respondent at his garden in Totnes and then this respondent asked him to relate unto him the actions he had seen between the said Prince and Mary Southcote. And to tell him the very truth and no more than what was really true. And what he would swear if he were thereunto called.

Then the said Tucker told this respondent that looking into Angel's window he saw Mr Prince and Mary Southcote in such a posture and he verily believed they had the carnal knowledge of each other's body. And that he saw her coats up nigh to her middle. And Mr Prince clasping her with his hands, saying to her *'(Child), you must bear or heave up your body towards me'*, or to that effect. And heard Mr Prince desire her to come to his house the next morning very early for that he would be the first should be up in the family and would give her a signal thereof by laying some hay or straw at the door. And this he protested to this respondent (as in the presence of God), was the very truth and no more than what he saw and heard and seemed to be much troubled at the seeing and hearing of it.

Elizabeth Payne

the wife of William Payne of Totnes in the county of Devon,
clothier, 46 years old.

To the first article, she answers that the articulate Mr Prince at present is and hath been for several years last past generally reputed a Priest in Holy Orders and Vicar of the parish of Berry Pomeroy for several years last past.

To the third article, she answers that about three or four months since (as near as this deponent can guess at the time) her fellow witness John Tucker being in this deponent's house in an evening went from her house to speak with John Angel having (as he said) some business with him. And having been waiting about a quarter of an hour, he returned again to this deponent's house and seemed to be under a great concern and trembling. And said to this deponent that he wished he had not gone out of her house that night which put this deponent into a trembling too, supposing there had been some murder committed, then this deponent asked him what it was, then the said Tucker told this deponent that Mr Prince and the young Thomas Southcote's daughter were at Angel's house and together. And that they were there in a very indecent posture and that he saw her coats up and Mr Prince very uncivil with her. And thereupon this deponent went from the said Tucker and he struck up into a chamber of this deponent's house where were her previous fellow witnesses Walter Bogan esquire, Mr Nicholas Gay, Edward Rounsevall and one Mr Edward Symonds. And in some short time after they all (excepting Mr Symons) went down to the said Angel's house but whether all together or not she cannot tell, she being about her business in the under rooms of her house. And about the same time that the said Tucker came and acquainted this deponent (as before she hath declared) her fellow witness William Amyott came also to this deponent's house and told this deponent that Mr Prince and Mary Southcote were at Angel's house together in a very indecent posture. And that her coats were up and he saw her thighs but this deponent being a woman did not ask many questions about it.

But sometime afterwards that evening this deponent being troubled at the said report went down to the said Angel's door where were some people gathered together looking in at a parlour window. And thereupon this deponent stepped up on a bench in the porch of the said Angel's door and looked in at the window through a quarrel of glass broken. And there saw Mr Prince sitting on a form in the said room and the girl standing close to him with his arm sometime about her neck and sometime about her waist, kissing of her. And this deponent saw him kiss her three or four times.

And this deponent being troubled at seeing it stepped off the bench and went into the entry and knocked at the ceiling or partition between the entry and the parlour where the said Mr Prince and Mary Southcote were. And at the same time the said Mr Gay called into the window saying *'Fye, Fye, for shame Mr Prince'*. Upon which Mary Southcote came out of the room and went out into the street and went over the bridge towards her home. And the people in the street shouting and hollering after her. But the said Mr Prince tarried sometime after her. Then this deponent spake to the said Mr Prince saying he might be ashamed to do these things, or to that effect. But the said Mr Prince did not answer her a word.

And so this deponent came away and went to her own house. And some few days after within the space of a week Thomas Southcote (the said Mary Southcote's father) came to this deponent's house being very well acquainted with this deponent. And then this deponent and the said Thomas Southcote did have some discourse about the report that was risen out of Mr Prince and his daughter being at Angel's house and the said Thomas Southcote then told this deponent that the next day after the said Mr Prince and his daughter had met at Angel's house the said Mr Prince came to his house. And there confessed to him that he played the fool with his daughter and kissed her and felt her, but that she had her virginity as for him.

And therefore willed her not to leave her church, nor to forsake the markets but to face them. But the said Thomas Southcote told the said Mr Prince (as he said to this deponent) that he had ruined his daughter or to that effect. And then said to this deponent that he wondered how Mr Prince could have the impudence to come to his house and own [up to] such things. And that if Mr Prince gave his daughter five hundred pounds he could not make her reparation or to that effect. And after this and some other discourse to this purpose, they parted.

To the fourth interrogatory, she answers that after the premise there was a public fame or report within the town of Totnes that the said Mr Prince and Mary Southcote had been naught [wicked] together at the said Angels' house at the time aforesaid. Everybody almost discoursing of it.

To the additional article, she answers that the said Mr Prince hath been for many years last past and at present is a married man and his wife is generally reputed a very pious, good virtuous woman and very courteous and obliging.

•

To the first interrogatory, she answers that she was summoned to appear to give her evidence in this cause but hath not received, been promised or expects any reward for giving her evidence.

To the second interrogatory, she answers that she hath not been taught or instructed by any person what or how to say or depose in this cause.

To the third interrogatory, she answers that her previous fellow witness John Tucker is bailiff of the hundred and doth commonly execute warrants and arrest people. And is a person of rude behaviour in his tongue and addicted to swearing which is the worst property she knows by him. But of late years he is much reclaimed and she believes he would not take a false oath.

To the fourth interrogatory, she answers that it was lately reported in the town of Totnes that the said John Tucker's wife should report that she had catched her husband with another woman on a furse faggot but the said Tucker's wife denied it to this respondent.

To the fifth interrogatory, she answers that there was lately a report in Totnes that the said

John Tucker and one Hutchens in the interrogatories named had a quarrel on the road and that thereupon the said Hutchens left his horse on the road and went away another way.

To the fourteenth interrogatory, she answers that she was never persuaded or threatened to give her evidence in this cause nor was ever in any person's garden about it.

To the fifteenth interrogatory, she answers that when this respondent saw Mr Prince and Mary Southcote together as before she hath deposed she was then standing up against him and believes they did not, whilst this respondent saw them, commit any Carnal Act. But that if any such thing were done between them it was before this respondent came they having been there a long time before.